T0145141

THE SUNSHINE CAPER

LOOKING FOR TREASURE ON
LONG BEACH ISLAND

By

Molly, Emma, and Caroline Schreier; Maggie Hennessey;
Gracie and Ellie O'Meara; Lucy O'Meara
ed. Richard Michael O'Meara

Illustrations by: Charleen Leslie

THE SUNSHINE CAPER
LOOKING FOR TREASURE ON LONG BEACH ISLAND

iUniverse books may be ordered through booksellers or by contacting:

iUniverse
1663 Liberty Drive
Bloomington, IN 47403
www.iuniverse.com
844-349-9409

Illustrations by Charleen Leslie
Copyright Richard M. O'Meara
www.richardomeara.com

ISBN: 978-1-6632-5081-0 (sc)
ISBN: 978-1-6632-5082-7 (e)

Library of Congress Control Number: 2023902883

Print information available on the last page.

iUniverse rev. date: 04/21/2023

DEDICATION

TO ALL THE NANAS AND POPPOPS, MOMS AND DADS
WHO MAKE SUMMERS AT THE SHORE SO MAGICAL

THE SUNSHINE CAPER

LOOKING FOR TREASURE ON LONG BEACH ISLAND

Before the boys showed up there were seven cousins who lived upstairs in the summer at Nana's house at the shore. The girls lived on the second floor and the boys lived in the kids' room out back. Everybody could keep their towels, their boogie boards, their wet bathing suits, buckets and shovels, their wagons and their umbrellas near the shower on the side of the house. And they spent most of their days on the beach riding the waves, digging holes, playing with their phones, and making sure Lucy didn't wander off. She was only six that summer after all and sometimes she thought she saw her mother down the beach and wandered off to take a look.

Molly and Emma were kind of in charge since they were the oldest and getting ready to leave for college that summer. Most of the time the rest of the cousins, Maggie, Caroline, Gracie, Ellie, and Lucy went along with what they said since the twins had spent lots of summers at the shore, knew their way around, and if they said they would mind the crew, the parents would pretty much let them all travel the island. They could use the bus and go to the shops and stop for donuts, go to Melt Down, the local ice cream place, and the Beach Haven Wawa.

All the girls were together for three weeks in Beach Haven Terrace. Their parents had dropped them off and left them in Nana's care and gone back to their jobs in the city. The boys were in camps, the parents were at work and Nana and the girls had Beach Haven pretty much to themselves.

"Ok ladies…make your beds, clean up those dishes and then up to the beach," said Nana from the bottom of the stairs. "I'll be at the Acme to get us some dinner and then I'll see you next to the lifeguard on the left…Molly and Em, make sure everybody swims right in front of the lifeguard. Keep an eye on Lucy. Everybody… listen to your cousins or I'm not going to be able to let you up to the beach by yourselves."

"Listen to your cousins," Caroline mumbled the words under her breath as she picked up a pillow and threw it at Gracie. Molly and Emma were her sisters and she had been told to listen to them since she was very little. In a way she was looking forward to them going away to school. She would finally be independent without older sisters looking over her shoulder and telling her what to do.

"Yes Nana," everybody bellowed down the stairs. "Yes Nana," Lucy laughed, catching up. "We'll be good." Everybody laughed at Lucy, picked up the rest of the pillows and blankets and started to get ready for the beach.

Only eight houses from the dune, it was an easy walk except when they brought all their stuff. Lucy sat in the wagon surrounded by folding chairs, a couple of buckets, five towels, and the umbrella. Maggie carried a small cooler full of juice boxes and pretzels and Ellie bounced a ball. Molly waited at the corner to make sure everybody watched for traffic before they crossed the road and Gracie played with her phone as she followed the crowd. Soon they were at the top of the dune looking down the long beach. "Wow," Caroline exclaimed. She was always amazed at how wide the beach was, how the sun reflected off the water and how hot the sand was. They kicked off their sandals, left them in a pile and started unloading the wagon. Lucy started running towards the lifeguard stand. "Here we go!" she yelled, spreading her arms and pretending to fly. "Here we go!"

They set up their stuff under the umbrella and ran down to the waves. Everybody got wet right away except for Lucy who still didn't trust the surf…but she got her feet wet and jumped up and down as the water washed in and out. After a while, Emma and Molly came out and spread their blankets over the hot sand. Soon the rest followed and they were nestled in a circle, watching the waves and the broad ocean that spread out before them.

"How much food do you think you would need to make it to Spain?" Ellie asked. She knew that on the other side of the ocean was Spain, a country full of castles and knights and flamenco dancers. "How far do you suppose it is?"

"Depends on what kind of boat you have," Molly said as she spread sunscreen on herself and on Lucy's back. "I'd want a pretty big boat."

"With a big engine," Maggie commented. "And a great big cabin in the back for sleeping and keeping our stuff dry."

"We would need a kitchen too," Gracie noted. Gracie was always concerned with lunch. "We would have to make a lot of sandwiches and maybe cook all the fish we'd catch."

"What do you think, a sailboat or a motor boat?" Molly asked. Everybody went quiet and looked out into the waves. In their minds each could see a different kind of boat, some with big sails and pennants flying in the wind. Other boats bounced up and down in the waves with small smokestacks painted black, big cabins and bright colored stripes on the sides.

"We gotta have a name!," Lucy suddenly remembered. "Our boat can't go to Spain without a name." She looked at Maggie and whispered, "Maggie, where's Spain again?"

Maggie pointed out into the water. "Way over there, way over there. Beyond the bouncing waves, beyond the clouds and the seagulls. Beyond all of that. As far as you can see and more. As far as you can imagine."

"Just over the horizon," Caroline piped in. "Where the earth curves like a big ball. On the other side of that." Caroline had studied the earth in engineering class. She could see the whole planet in her mind as it turned and spun around the sun.

"We're going to need a lot of sandwiches," Lucy concluded.

"*Dreams*," Ellie said. "*Dreams* is a good name."

"*Dreams* is a good name," Gracie said. "But how about *cousins? The Seven Cousins.* We'd be like pirates heading out…not knowing how far we were going or how long it would take us to get there."

"Or maybe just *Magic,*" Ellie decided. "*Magic.*" Everybody stopped talking and just stared out into the blue water. It was so big, it stretched so far from top to bottom, left to right, up and down. The whole ocean was magic and they all just stared, Molly to Lucy…all of them.

After a while, Caroline rolled over in the sand and stood up. "I'm going to look for shells…anybody want to come along?"

Lucy jumped up, Ellie got her bucket and Maggie decided to go too. Molly, Emma and Gracie were playing with their phones. "You guys go ahead," Molly said. "We'll catch up…Don't go too far."

Lucy ran ahead and found a bunch of mussel shells, all black and slimy. There were white clam shells a bit further, and Lucy kept following the trail, past a bit of seaweed, past a bit of wood, past a crab which scampered into the water…and just past a green bottle half buried in the sand.

Caroline stopped at the bottle and pulled it out of the sand. The bottle was green and slippery. It had clearly been in the ocean for a long time. The bottle still had its cork, and there was a label which was old and rotting. "I wonder what this is?" Caroline asked.

"Let's open it up," Maggie said. "Let's look inside." By now the four youngest were all gathered around the bottle. They waited for Molly, Emma and Gracie to catch up.

Caroline handed the bottle to Emma and watched as she tried to remove the cork. It wouldn't budge. "Break the glass," Maggie suggested. "Hurry, I want to see what is inside!"

Emma tried again. She put part of her t-shirt around the bottle and held on with both hands. Molly grabbed the cork.

"Now twist!" And twist they did. All of a sudden after a good deal of grunting and slipping the cork began to move. Slowly at first. Lucy was jumping up and down with anticipation. Ellie did a backflip. Maggie was holding on to Emma. They twisted and turned, and finally at the last minute the cork popped out, the bottle fell into the sand and Maggie and Emma fell on their backs.

They all stared at the bottle wondering what was inside. They stared for a long time, listening to the ocean, listening to the seagulls squawking over the water. They all heard a strange sound as if a storm was inside the bottle just waiting to get out. And then the storm stopped and there was silence.

Maggie looked at Ellie and Caroline. Gracie put her arm around Lucy. Molly looked at Emma with a questioning look, reached inside the bottle with one finger and slowly eased out a rolled up crusty piece of brown paper with a ribbon around it. "This is old," Emma whispered. "This is very old."

"Read it! Read it," Maggie said. "What's it say?"

Emma unrolled the paper, held it in two hands and began to read:

> **Greetings: To those who receive this document, greetings. We are the crew of the good ship The Augustina, a fair sloop out of Beach Haven, trading with the good people of Tenerife in the Canary Islands. If you are reading this it means we are lost…lost in a foul wind out of the west as we proceeded to our home in Spain. We are**

lost with nothing left behind except a small important treasure, a joy for whoever has the faith to believe in us and search for it. The secret will go to those who follow the clues and travel the road to the end.

The first clue is blue.
Go to the Light House, climb all the way
Search for the window that looks out on the bay.
We wish you well on the journey; believe in us and adieu.

"Wow," exclaimed Caroline. "I mean double wow. What do you suppose this means?" Everybody was excited. But none of them really knew what to make of the message.

"You suppose it's real?" Gracie whispered.

"Maybe it's gold," Lucy exclaimed.

"A stash of candy," Ellie guessed, with a smile on her face.

"Or a bunch of gift cards!" Maggie thought out loud.

"Tickets to the Surflight to see a secret performance," Emma said. She looked like she might start to sing.

"Who knows," Molly laughed, "but I'll bet it's something special. You guys want to go searching for it?"

"Yessssss!" they all agreed, talking over each other. "We can take the bus to Barnegat Light this afternoon. Let's do it!" And, as quickly as they could, the girls picked up their stuff, packed it all into the wagon, gathered up their sandals and headed home.

The girls reached the house, sticky with sunscreen and salt and sand. "Hose off, ladies!" Emma said in her best General voice. Gracie took the hose, spraying the sand off of everyone's feet. Maggie, though, was thinking ahead. "I get the shower first!" Cries of "me, next!" followed. A line assembled outside of the outdoor shower.

Molly, however, was willing to bend the rules. She tiptoed up the stairs to the off-limits upstairs bathroom to shower. Ellie, always a keen observer, followed, sensing an opportunity. "What are YOU up to?" Ellie said, looking up at Molly with her big eyes.

Molly, realizing she had been caught, smiled. "Alright, Ellie. If you don't say anything, you can use this shower after me too." Ellie took Molly's hand and shook it, happy with their deal.

Once the showers were over, the outfits picked out, and the aloe applied, the girls assembled outside the house in the afternoon sun. "Women! And you are my women!" Molly said, imitating the voice their Pop Pop, a retired General, used whenever he meant business. "To the bus stop! Careful on the sidewalk! Someone take Lucy's hand!"

The group made their way down the block and to the corner to wait for the shuttle. Molly stood on the edge, ensuring no one got too close to the road.

"It's coming!" Lucy cried. The bus pulled to a slow stop in front of them. The bus driver, a kind-looking old man with many wrinkles from smiles and the sun, opened the door, greeting each girl as she entered. The girls filled the first three rows, glancing back at the few other kids and teenagers sitting spread out through the rest of the bus.

"Alright, we're gonna take this all the way to the end," Gracie said, sitting back in her seat and pulling up Instagram on her phone.

Maggie, taking a peek at the phone over Gracie's shoulder, soon snatched the phone from Grace's hands. "Look, it's a boy!"

The girls focused in, trying to get any information they could out of Gracie—and when she wouldn't speak, Ellie. The girls gossiped, begging for details, and making them up when they didn't know them. Giving Grace a funny look, Emma said, "I bet his name is Bartholomew."

Lucy jumped into the conversation, moving up and down on her bus seat. "Or maybe Bert!" As the girls brainstormed possible names for Grace's mystery beau, the northern half of the island slipped past the windows of the bus. Maggie shouted out, "I bet it's Javier!" just as the bus slowed to a stop.

"It's the lighthouse! It's our stop!" Ellie cried. The girls nimbly slipped out of their seats, thanking the bus driver and walking back out into the sunlight. Once gathered outside the bus, the girls followed a gravel path through the trees. They came upon a rocky beach, the red and white lighthouse directly ahead.

The wind whipped through their hair as they began jogging towards the light house, Caroline and Lucy racing. "I'm winning!" Lucy gleefully cried, Caroline smiling as she reached down to tickle her.

They reached the base of the lighthouse and waited as Molly and Emma tried to count the correct amount of change for seven tickets to the top. Soon they were inside, staring up at the impossibly long circular staircase. "Let's gooooo!" shouted Caroline, leading the girls up the staircase, followed by Emma, Gracie, Maggie, Ellie, Lucy, and Molly.

The stairs took quite a long time. They took breaks at the landings, looking out the windows to the water below. "This sure is a lot of stairs," Lucy commented at the second to last landing. They were almost there.

With a lot of huffing and puffing, they reached the top. "You can see the whole island," Gracie said, looking around in wonder. They moved towards the railings, walking around the perimeter of the top to see the island from all directions. They looked at the beach and the tops of houses, seeing how they got smaller and smaller. They looked at the ocean, the sun glinting off the waves for miles and miles. And Molly looked at her cousins, counting them over and over, and making sure no one got too close to the railing.

After looking out for a while, Maggie started looking at the lighthouse itself. Facing the bay, she looked up at the light, wondering how to climb to the very top. A streak of light caught her eye. There was a blue bottle, wedged between the ceiling of the structure and the metal railing. "Guys, look, the clue!"

The cousins gathered around, looking up. "Give me a boost!" Molly and Caroline lifted Maggie up so that she could just reach the tip of the glass bottle. With a shaky hand, Maggie grasped the bottle as she was lowered back to the floor. "Guys, help me pull the top off!"

Ellie grabbed the cork as Maggie held onto the bottle, Gracie and Emma holding onto Maggie and Molly anxiously guarding the edge. They pulled and pulled, and just as a burst of wind blew through, the cork came out with a pop. Molly caught

Ellie as she fell against her while Maggie juggled the bottle. Everyone reached out their hands. Caroline caught the bottle before it fell to the ground, but the note slipped through, catching on the wind and floating over the side.

"Noooooo!!!" The girls exclaimed, clutching the railing and watching as the old, tattered paper fell down, down, down. It traveled south along the water, following the long line of rocks bordering the ocean before settling on some brush far down the beach.

The girls looked at each other, disappointed with the early end of their quest. Except Lucy. Pointing her arm over the edge to the beach, she shouted with her strong little voice, "LET'S GO GET IT!"

The girls rallied around their youngest member, shouting their support as they moved to race down the stairs. The trip down took much less time, the pitter patter of their feet echoing through the lighthouse.

With more huffing and puffing, they burst back into the sunlight. "IT'S THIS WAY!!" Lucy screamed, breaking into a run. The girls followed her down the concrete path parallel to the beach.

They reached the metal bars at the end of the pavement path. The ocean stretched to their left, the beach to their right, and a line of black rocks directly in front of them. "Guys, I think I see it!" Emma said, pointing to the shrubs on the beach. "Let's go on the rocks!"

"Alright, but we have to watch the waves!" Molly said, eyeing the slippery rocks. Looking back at the girls, she said, "I'll go first! Everybody hold onto each other!"

She slipped through the metal bars onto the rocks, found her footing, and reached up to help the next girl through. One by one they climbed down onto the rocks. Excited with the adrenaline of their adventure, they hopped along the rocks, jumping over gaps and dodging splashes of water from waves underneath.

Soon, they could see the bushes directly across from them, on the other side of a strip of water that divided them from a sandy strip of beach. Maggie looked down at the water between the rocks and the beach. She eyed a spot where the gap was small a bit further ahead. She raced ahead of the pack of cousins, and without pausing to think, jumped over the water to the beach, just barely landing on her feet. "This way!" She yelled.

The cousins followed. Grace and Ellie leapt over the water with the grace of ballerinas. Caroline jumped like she was hugging the sky, reaching her hands high to feel the salty air. Emma jumped next, her long legs easily touching down on the beach. Emma loved to climb on rocks. She grinned.

Last were Molly and Lucy. Both girls giggling, Molly gathered up the smallest cousin in her arms, Lucy clinging tightly to her neck. Lucy clicked her tongue, striking out a kind of a rallying cry. Molly picked up the beat, and the cousins on the other side joined in. When Molly jumped, Emma caught them on the other side.

"Guys, we found it!" Ellie shouted. Molly, Emma, and Lucy sprinted across the beach to the cousins already gathered in a circle around a bush, Gracie holding the note in her hands. She read aloud:

> *Congratulations: You climbed all the stairs*
> *And looked out at an island so pretty and fair.*
> *The next clue is waiting, and it's really a treat;*
> *Just ask the waitress who sings the most sweet.*

The girls looked around at each other, thinking hard. Then their eyes fell upon Emma, who was jumping up and down in excitement.

"It's the Showplace! Let's go let's go, let's go!"

The wind sweeping through their hair, they started to follow Emma back towards the lighthouse, the torn clue grasped tightly in Molly's hand.

As the girls waited to board the bus, Emma and Gracie, the family theater nerds, chatted excitedly about their favorite musicals and the super-advanced theater trivia they might need to crack the clue. While they debated the merits of the most recent Surflight production, the other girls looked on, bored by their deep dive into Broadway. "No big deal," said Caroline. "We just have to go to the Show Place."

Emma and Gracie turned defensively on Caroline. Gracie fired back: "You never know." The Show Place was, after all, the ultimate combination of ice cream sundaes and musical theater. Emma nodded vigorously. Ellie, ready for a change of subject, did a back handspring and Lucy politely applauded.

With a sigh of relief, Maggie pointed out that the bus was approaching. Molly herded everyone up and distributed the bus fare. The bus driver welcomed the girls back with a kind smile, and they sat, glad to get out of the sun. Their respite from the heat, however, did not last long. About halfway back across the island, the bus began making strange noises. After a brief struggle, the bus driver pulled over and gradually sputtered to a stop. "Sorry folks, looks like this is the last stop for a while," the bus driver announced. "I would get off here- I'm not sure how long it's gonna take to get the bus up and running again."

The cousins exited the bus and milled in the crowd for a while, wondering what to do. Nana and Pop-pop were at work. They didn't want to disturb them, but the girls were much too far from the Show Place to walk. As Molly and Caroline figured out how much it would be to call a Lyft, Emma scanned her surroundings and found the solution to their dilemma. "Ladies, follow me," she called over her shoulder, walking in the direction of a canopy that read, "The Surf Buggy Bike Shop."

Emma marched right up to the employee standing next to the shop under an umbrella. To this kid of no more than fourteen, she said: "My good sir, I would like the finest tandem bike that money can buy. And by finest, I mean cheapest." Molly rolled her eyes. Emma may have been dramatic, but it was true and they should probably get used to it. Cheap was the way to go for both sisters these days, who would soon be broke college students.

Five minutes later the girls were situated in a beautiful tandem bike. With Molly, Maggie, and Ellie in the back row, and Emma, Lucy, Caroline, and Gracie in the front, the cousins were ready for the six-mile journey ahead of them. Caroline, a dedicated athlete, shouted out in her best soccer coach voice, "Is everyone ready to work?" It was hot, and it had already been a long day. But they were ready to find the next clue.

Lucy was of course exempt, as her legs did not reach the pedals, but she cheered enthusiastically, nonetheless. With that, they set off, pedaling in sync down quiet back roads, protected from the sun by the red and white striped awning over their heads. Emma, fresh from Driver's Ed, sat at the steering wheel, but not without complaint from some of her cousins. Granted, she did hit the curb and a fire hydrant and run into a stop sign, but she was doing her best.

While the cousins were all troopers, around mile four some of the group began to tire. Maggie, claiming dehydration, took an extended beverage break and enjoyed the sea breeze in her hair as she sipped a Capri Sun from Molly's bag. Gracie's dancer legs, while strong, also began to slow. Ellie, already an accomplished gymnast for her age, pedaled furiously, and refused to slow down, but was sweating buckets. Lucy dozed in the front, leaning on Caroline's lap.

They needed a break. Luckily, the girls were passing through Bay Village and stopped at the water ice stand for water and a refreshing mid-morning Italian Ice.

After Ellie had declared, and the group confirmed, that cotton candy was indeed the best flavor, the girls returned to the tandem bike. "We're only a mile away!" shouted Emma, riding a sugar rush and pedaling fast.

"Let's gooooooo!" screamed Lucy, laughing as the bike picked up speed.

"I can't feel my legs!!!!!!!!" Ellie cackled, a crazy look in her eyes.

In a matter of minutes, the tandem bike pulled up to the Show Place.

Caroline set Lucy on her feet and Molly made Ellie down a water bottle. Maggie hopped off the bike, expertly tousled her hair, and moved to the window. Nose pressed against the window, she announced, "It's empty. I think it's closed." Gracie ran to the door where crowds lined up every night, eager to get inside, and tentatively pulled the handle. It did not budge.

Gracie slumped against the wall. "What are we going to do now?" Eager to help, Lucy pulled on the door with all of her might, but alas, it remained locked. Emma was not yet ready to give up. If they waited until the Show Place was open, they would lose daylight, and would not be able to find the treasure. As a last ditch attempt, Emma walked over to the back door. The familiar mural of a waiter, saying "Auf Wiedersein, goodnight," greeted them. They all remembered the mural and the bittersweet sight of that last candy-striped waiter, frozen smiling at the end of a Showplace show. Emma tugged half-heartedly at the door, her eyes widening when she met no resistance. She shouted to the other girls, who cheered in response and hurried over. They filed into the cool building.

The search for the clue began. Ellie and Caroline decided to search the ice cream freezers, delighting in the rows of fresh, untouched ice cream. Gracie studied the playbills mounted on the wall, shouting to the other girls when she recognized a cast member from visits over the years. Maggie checked under the tables, finding only the occasional piece of gum. Lucy rifled through the hat box reserved for customers celebrating birthdays, trying on a cowboy hat, and then a baby bonnet.

Molly and Emma stood in the center of the room. There had to be something they were forgetting. They racked their brains for Show Place knowledge that they had acquired from a lifetime of "Oliver's Twist" sundaes. Suddenly, a light bulb went off in Emma's brain.

"What is it that they always say about the waiters at the beginning of the show?" Emma asked, pacing.

Lucy called out to them happily from under a gigantic pirate's hat. She'd found a patch too, and had it precariously pulled over one eye. "They match the wallpaper!" She threw a pile of hats up into the air like confetti.

The older girls rushed to the walls and began to feel carefully for a clue. Soon enough, Caroline discovered a red and white striped envelope that matched the wallpaper exactly. Everyone crowded around her as she pulled out a delicate-looking piece of paper.

Caroline started to read it, but Maggie interrupted her. "blah blah blah blah where are we going Caroline?"

They all crowded around, reading in silence.

> *Avast ye seekers, walk the plank, never fear*
> *No ill fate meets a landlubber who files off that pier*
> *Let Kokomo carry ye o'er sapphire crests*
> *While the renters with coladas do their Electric Slide bests*
>
> *As the sun drops beneath you, the day melting to gold*
> *You'll shiver, me timbers, not from feeling the cold*
> *Make way for the jewel that isn't on land*
> *where thar be silly songs with a snack and drink stand*

"Does that mean what I think it means?" Ellie asked, a wide grin spreading across her face.

"It can only mean one thing: The Black Pearl!" Grace yelled. When Lucy looked at her, not understanding, Grace picked her up and spun her around. "It's a boat, Lucy! Remember the boat on the bay? We went with Nana and Pop-Pop once. There's a dance floor, and pizza, and a D.J. who'll play Taylor Swift and BTS all night!"

Lucy shrieked in delight. "WE ARE NEVER EVER EVER / GETTING BACK TOGETHER" she sang, pumping her arms above her head. The other girls laughed, and Grace took her hands, pulling her back and forth.

Emma checked her watch. "The sunset cruise leaves from the dock in Beach Haven in an hour! My phone died, but Molly, if we can catch Pop Pop on his way home from the Coast Guard, I bet he'll give us a ride to the dock!"

Molly was already dialing before Emma had finished her sentence. Ellie and Maggie twirled in circles, their sundresses swirling around them in great plumes of color, while Caroline leaned close to Lucy.

"Shiver me timbers, argggh, methinks the treasure be gettin' close," she growled, in her best pirate voice. Lucy began to laugh and jump up and down.

Molly called them to the front door of Faria's. "We're in luck! Pop-Pop is just driving onto the island now. He said he'd take us to the dock if we don't mind crowding in, but he's just going to drop us because he's got to head to Beach Haven Fishery before he and Nana head out for dinner."

The girls walked together arm in arm to the Boulevard, singing the chorus of more than a few Taylor Swift songs as they reached the curb. Sure enough, in just a few minutes, a black Jeep pulled up, and the window rolled down. A deeply tanned arm waved. Their grandfather was wearing an Eagles cap pulled low over his forehead. His eyes, barely visible, were the color of the ocean.

"If it isn't the sunshine crew," he said. "Whatcha all been up to today? Lazy day at the beach?"

Ellie started to protest, but Grace gave her a warning look before locking eyes with Molly and Emma. Molly took the hint. "Yeah," said Molly. "Pretty lazy beach day. Same old, same old." She winked at Lucy, and Maggie squeezed the littlest treasure-seeker's hand.

Pop-Pop nodded. "I hope you girls aren't saying you're bored. The island always has a little magic ready for you, even on a regular beach day, right Lu?" He patted the six year old on the head. Lucy nodded, trying to keep her face super serious. But Ellie's face turned pink. "It's not like we're chasing buried treasure or anything!" She blurted.

Molly looked startled, but then recovered. "Ellie, you've been thinking about those chocolate covered doubloons from the arcade all day!" she said to the petite candy-lover. Ellie smiled with relief, realizing she hadn't given anything away, and did a round-off before hopping into the car.

Molly and Emma rode together in the front, and Maggie, Caroline, Grace and Ellie all piled into the back, with Lucy on Maggie's lap.

Before they knew it, they were back in Beach Haven, approaching the towering ferris wheel at Fantasy Island. Another pirate ship, the swinging Sea Dragon ride, rose above them, flashing bright neon lights as the sun sank lower in the sky behind it. When Pop-Pop pulled over near the Black Pearl's dock, he gave the girls each a $5 bill "for adventurin'" as he put it. With his gift, Emma calculated that they'd all have enough for the sunset cruise.

It was crowded on board. The cousins stayed together by holding hands in a chain as they zigzagged across the deck. Caroline led the way and found a little spot under the D.J.'s booth for all of them to stand. In front of them was the dance floor, and beyond, a Tiki bar, with a thatched roof awning. Large clusters of bananas towered on either side of the counter.

The other passengers were mostly adults, wearing wide-brimmed sun hats and a lively mix of Hawaiian shirts. As the D.J. welcomed the passengers to the ship, goblets of orange, pink and blue drinks garnished with pineapple and cherries floated over Lucy's head as they were passed by servers. Grace, noticing the little girl licking her lips, maneuvered her way to the bar and came back with a tray full of seven lemonades and seven hot dogs. Before the first song, "Dancing Queen," had even ended, they'd devoured it all. The cousins were so excited about the hunt they hadn't realized how hungry they were.

The thrum of "Shake it Up" blared from the music booth above them. Ellie jumped in the air, delighted. But Maggie looked worried. "How are we EVER going to find a clue here?" She muttered.

"Let's spread out," Emma said. "We'll pair up. Ellie and I will check the other side of the boat. Molly, you and Maggie see what you can find on this side. And Grace, can you see if you can check the crow's nest with Lucy? She's so little, no one will suspect if she climbs up a few steps!"

Grace nodded. "Aye aye! Got it. Let's meet back here in fifteen minutes." She grabbed Lucy's hand, and the two of them made their way across the deck towards the rope ladder under the schooner's tattered black flag, ripping in the wind.

A half an hour later, the girls sat defeated on the cargo trunks in the middle of the ship. While "Get This Party Started!" pounded out of the speakers, Maggie twirled her hair listlessly in her fingers.

"We haven't found ANYTHING—and the boat is almost back to shore," Ellie cried.

"I'm sure it's here" Caroline mumbled. "It's the "*jewel that isn't on land.*" She sighed. "The pearl. It just has to be!"

At that moment, the music suddenly stopped, with a screech. The boat's passengers groaned, and a lady wearing a Showplace t-shirt and bright red lipstick called out, "Hey, no fair! We're not even at the dock yet!"

There was a crackle over the loudspeaker. "HEY HEY HEY sea lovers! We almost forgot, tonight we have a very special dedication to play, for a group of ladies who loovvvvve the pirate's life! Augustina, if you're out there, here's your special request for the "sunshine girls!" Once again, the speaker crackled, and a voice cut through the orange and pink streaked sky. There were no instruments in the beginning, just a voice.

Daaaaayyyyyyyyyyy-o! Dayyyyyyyyyy-o.

The girls all stared at each other. Lucy didn't recognize the song—but as she listened, she did think the words were funny.

> *Come Mister Tally Man, tally me banana*
> *(Daylight come and we want go home)*
> *Come Mister Tally Man, tally me banana*
> *(Daylight come and we want go home)*

"Augustina," Molly whispered. "Why does that sound so familiar?"

Emma looked up from her phone. "I know this song," she said. It's by Harry Belafonte. But…" she frowned. "Why did the d.j. say "sunshine girls?"

Maggie grabbed her cousin by the arm. "Don't you see!" She shouted. "It's us! We're the sunshine girls!"

Caroline's eyes drifted to her littlest cousin. Lucy was stomping to the beat of the song and seemed to have caught a second wind after the disappointment of the search. Suddenly, her eyes opened so wide that Ellie could see the ocean reflected back in them.

"BANANAS." Lucy said. "BANANAS!!!!!!!"

Ellie patted her on the arm. "It's been a long day, Luce. I know."

Lucy smacked her hand away. "NOOOOO!!!! She shrieked, jumping to her feet. "BANANAS!!!" The girl pointed towards the bar, as the music swelled around them.

> *Lift 6 foot, 7 foot, 8 foot bunch*
> *(Daylight come and we want go home)*
> *6 foot, 7 foot, 8 foot bunch*
> *(Daylight come and we want go home)*

Before anyone knew what was happening, Lucy had shimmied up Emma's shoulders and was steering her towards the Tiki counter. The other cousins ran to catch up.

In front of them were the two towers of bananas. You might say that each was at least 6, 7, or maybe even 8 feet high.

"Oh em gee!" Grace sighed. "Bananas! It must be here! Do you think there's a clue underneath? And who the heck is Augustina?"

"We can't worry about that now," Molly cautioned. "Quick, while the bartender is on the dance floor—let's get these bananas up!"

Each girl took hold of a bunch of bananas and slowly—as if they were moving a Jenga tower—lifted the cluster of bananas in the air. And sure enough, there under the counter, was a single banana leaf: with writing on it.

Lucy grabbed it and read it aloud from her perch on Emma's shoulders.

Day-o! Bravo!
The sun is setting
And you're almost done with this quest, I'm betting
Daybreak comes and you want to go home

But there's one last beach you'll need to comb.
1880, it 'twas when Augustina vanished by Monmouth beach
Her treasures, they floated to just within reach.
At low tide take Ohio to the dunes you know well
Bring a paddle board with you past the ocean's swell

When the tallest among you can't stand anymore
Send her down, to the sandy ocean's dark floor
It may seem at first to be a trap of some kind
Believe us, we're rooting for you, the treasure to find!

Lucy looked around. For once, no one said a word, they all just looked at each other. Molly finally broke the silence.

"Augustina! Augustina was the name of the ship in the first clue!" And Augustina was the name the D.J. said—it was *Augustina* who requested the banana song!"

Caroline shook her head. "And the *Augustina* must have disappeared on Monmouth beach, back in…." She consulted the banana leaf. "1880! Didn't the first clue say it was a ship from Spain?"

Emma smiled. "You're right! Maybe we weren't so far off when we were all daydreaming on the beach this morning about Spain, across the ocean."

Only Lucy looked unhappy. "What are we waiting for?" She said, motioning toward the pier. The boat was already pulling into the dock. "We've got to get to the beach!"

***

The sun was setting. Seven shadowy figures wheeled two beach carts across Beach Road and up the street past the last dark houses on Ohio Avenue before the dunes. Balanced between the two carts was a long, pink paddleboard--Maggie's mother's---which she kept in the crawlspace under Nana and Pop-Pop's house. It had been more than a little scary retrieving it from its shadowy resting place under the house, where it rested with its family of dozens of boogie boards and skimboards, used by all the cousins for countless summers. In the end, it had been Ellie and Lucy, the smallest girls, who had found it, and pushed it to the opening so that Molly and Emma could hoist it on the carts.

Each of these boards had carried the girls out on the waves hundreds of times, their own makeshift boats for learning the waves and exploring the ocean. And now, they were voyaging out, looking for the traces of other adventurers who'd come before them.

Everything was quiet, except for the smack of the girls' flip flops against the pavement. The moon was high in the sky now, blood orange and bursting. They were so close. Each of them was lost in her own thoughts, focused on the task ahead.

When they reached the highest point of the path over the dunes they kicked off their shoes. The sand, still balmy from the day's heat, warmed their feet. In the light of their flashlights they could see the sea before them: mostly dark except for the break, with its flashes of white, choppy foam.

Silently, they lifted the paddleboard, each of them taking a piece, and carried it towards the water.

Emma was all business. "Okay, you guys. You know the plan. Molly and I will be in the water. Grace, Caroline, you'll swim out holding the board, with Ellie, Maggie and Lucy on it. Once we get out there, Molly and I will swim to you. We need to stay directly in front of the path from Ohio--that's the only direction we have from the last clue. Molly and I can steer the paddleboard, and then we dive. Everybody got it?"

The other girls nodded. Lucy put her hand on the board. One by one, the other girls placed their hands on top of hers. "We got this!" Caroline whispered, smiling at her sisters and cousins, as they all fanned their arms back. Together, they waded into the waves.

The water was bracing. It took a moment for their bodies to get used to the temperature, and to swimming at night. Even up close, they couldn't always see the waves coming. But as the older girls swam out, they used the familiar sounds of the waves to judge each breaker's timing and size. It was a little colder and much darker, but still the ocean they knew.

After a few minutes, Caroline and Grace had pushed the paddleboard well past the break, where the ocean, except for the occasional nudge and sway, was calm.

Molly called to her cousin. "Can you stand there, Grace?"

"Nope," she said. "But maybe you can?" Molly, the tallest of them, just a hair taller than Emma, was a full head higher than Grace.

Molly swam over. "I'm touching now," she said. "Remember the clue. *When the tallest among you can't stand anymore.* We need to go deeper." Emma appeared next to her, and together, Grace, Molly and Emma pushed the board out further into the dark water.

Soon, Molly spoke. "Here!" she said. "I'm just past the point where I can't touch." Caroline and Grace steadied the paddleboard. For a moment, the board seemed to have a mind of its own. The current had caught it, dragging it away from the other girls. Maggie hopped off, and holding onto Emma's arm, pulled it back to the group.

Lucy and Ellie were quiet, too excited to speak. When Grace swept her flashlight over the younger girls, she could see her sister shivering. Ellie's face, though, was tense with concentration. With her arm on Lucy's back to steady her, she took advantage of the spotlight to rally her cousins.

"Let's do this thing!" she yelled.

Molly dove. After a few moments, she came up, shrugging.

"It's crazy dark," she said. "Hard to see anything at all. And I scraped my foot on something! A shell, or a piece of rock. I think I'm bleeding."

"I'm going too," Emma said. "Grace, watch the paddleboard."

Again and again the girls surfaced. Each time five other faces watched anxiously, waiting for them to emerge, and each time, the twins rose, empty handed. Finally, Molly turned to them, rubbing her foot.

"This isn't working," she said, treading water. "There's nothing down there. The only thing I've touched was that old crab shell, or whatever it was that cut me."

"We don't even know what we're looking for," Emma said. "Let's go back to the clue--what did it say exactly?"

Grace shrugged. "That the voyagers--that they're rooting for us. That it might seem like a trap, but there's a treasure down there."

Emma frowned. "So much for X marks the spot," she said, motioning around her. "No big deal, just check the ENTIRE ocean!" With a flop, she fell back into a frustrated back float, kicking her legs in front of her.

"HOOOOOOLD up, HOOOOOOOOOOOld up!" Caroline said, treading water nearby. "What did the clue say again? *You may think it's a trap of some kind.*"

"A trap…" Maggie murmured. "A trap! What if… what if that was the clue?"

Grace looked at her, confused. "What are you saying?"

The girls all leapt up into the night air as a breaker passed. The paddleboard bobbed up and away from them, but Caroline steadied it and returned her attention to Maggie, her face now illuminated by moonlight. "I mean," Maggie continued slowly. "I've been trying to imagine what we're actually looking for, and it can't be a treasure chest."

Emma bolted upright from her back float. "So what you're saying is, what if we're actually looking for *a trap*?"

"Maggie, you're a genius!" Molly said. "We must be looking for something on the seafloor! It's not a lobster trap. We learned in school about those, and they were usually made of wood. A trap made in 1880 wouldn't last this long. But a crab trap...that's a whole other story! I think they would have been using ring traps, made of steel, by the time the *Augustina* was around."

Lucy was cold, and shivering. They'd been on the water now for what seemed like hours--without the usual sun above their heads to keep them warm in the ocean's waves. But she wasn't even a little tired. She couldn't believe Molly knew all these things about lobsters and crabs, and ships from so long ago. Suddenly, she felt very brave.

"I'm going down there" she announced, pulling herself to a surfing position on the paddleboard.

"Whoa, surfer girl, you absolutely are not!" Emma said, pulling her into her arms. "Grace, you and Molly go. Now that we know what we're looking for, maybe we'll have better luck."

Both girls took a deep breath and dove down.

Grace shone her flashlight out into the dark waters behind them. The sea went on forever--much further, she knew than she could see, even on a sunny day. How many ships had sailed these waters? And what had happened to the *Augustina*, that last day back in 1880? Why had it never reached its New York port?

Emma surfaced. The other girls couldn't see her face, but they could hear the emotion in her voice. "We found something. It's a trap."

Molly's head popped up. She was breathing hard. "It's mostly buried under the sand. But there's definitely something there. It's made of steel. And it cut my foot before!"

Grace pushed the paddleboard towards Caroline. Three pairs of feet kicked up above the surface and then they were gone, as the three oldest girls dove down. Maggie pushed herself back onto the board and wrapped her arms around Lucy and Ellie to keep them warm. Again and again, the three girls dove, and surfaced. Finally, Molly emerged, triumphant.

"We've got it! Wait until you see THIS!"

All the cousins started shouting at once, asking questions. But Molly was underwater again, as a massive breaker hit the paddleboard, and Maggie and Caroline lunged to steady it.

But the ocean seemed to sense that the girls had work to do. The water calmed again, shape-shifting into a smooth, flat plane. It seemed to Lucy that the only sound now was her breathing.

Maggie shone the flashlight at the water in front of them. They all waited.

And then, they saw it. Rising above the surface with three sets of hands supporting it was a rusted crab trap. It looked a little like a wire basket but was long and shaped like a rectangle. Large barnacles clung to the sides and glowed like pearls in the light from Maggie's flashlight. Three heads surfaced alongside it, and while Grace, Emma and Molly heaved the large trap sideways onto the paddleboard, Maggie shifted the younger girls to one end, to make room.

In the center of the trap, was a round, clay vessel with a narrow lip. It was covered in a coat of bright green sea algae, and a few of the same baubles of barnacles that had clung to the trap. Caroline pulled the container out of the trap, as the girls crowded around. It was heavy, but with effort, she turned it partially upside down. Dozens of silver coins poured out. Ellie rubbed at several of the coins, rinsing them off. With the flashlight, they could see the words on the coins: "Dei Gratia 1821 Ferdinand VII." *For Ferdinand, by the grace of God.* Lucy started to laugh, taking them in her hands, and letting them run through her fingers, spilling onto the paddleboard. It was well after sunset, but the sunshine girls had found their treasure.

AFTERWORD

If you're on Long Beach Island and you find yourself at the east end of Ohio Avenue, take a few extra steps and climb onto the sandy path that winds up over the dunes to the beach. At the top, there's a bench. Take a minute. Maybe sit down. It's a steep dune, and once you've climbed it, you may need to catch your breath.

Your eyes will wander to the sea glittering in front of you. The sky is that mix of a pale butter yellow and the most startling blue you've ever seen. Everything shines. Look at the place where the water meets the sky. It's an important place. It's the place where ships, for centuries, have disappeared somewhere just out of sight, on their way to ports beyond.

The New Jersey Maritime Museum, located in Beach Haven, has records of all known shipwrecks in the state's history. Molly couldn't believe how easy it was: a simple keyword search online brought up a Spanish brig called the *Augustina* that had vanished in a storm in February of 1880 as she traveled from Havana to New York. The *Augustina* was, according to the database, "a total loss." No trace of the crew or passengers had ever been found.

Trade between Americans and the Spanish colonies was well-established by the *Augustina*'s time. According to the shipwreck database, the brig had been carrying cedar and animal skins. The girls' initial idea, that the *Augustina* had been a fishing boat, had been wrong: it was a cargo ship, used for trade. The trap the girls had found was probably the only one on board, used by the crew of eight to catch dinner during their long journey.

The coins they'd found--thirteen hundred and fifty two coins, to be exact--were *reales,* a Spanish currency used throughout Spain's colonies in the 19ᵗʰ-century. When the girls brought them to the museum in Beach Haven the day after they'd found them, the museum's curator nearly fell off her chair. The coins were going to be analyzed by conservators at the museum, and later, displayed. The hope was to gather enough information about the *Augustina* and its crew from other sources to create an exhibit about the brig.

You may also find yourself noticing a small stone set in the dune grass, in front of the bench you're sitting on. And if you do, take a moment to read it.

The O'Meara cousins honor the crew
Of the fair ***Augustina***
Lost February 3, 1880

The treasures found by the Sunshine Seven
June 15, 2019

How did the coins end up in a crab trap? Did the crew put them there when it became clear that the boat was in trouble, thinking they might be able to retrieve the coins later if they managed to survive? And who was it, exactly, who had left the girls those clues? I leave it to you, dear reader, to consider our story, and the possibilities, as you sit, the ocean in front of you, magical and vast.

Printed in the United States
by Baker & Taylor Publisher Services